D1238720

*This book was purchased
with funds from a
generous donation by*

Dr. Kathryn W. Davis

CALIFORNIA
MISSIONS

Discovering Mission San Rafael Arcángel

BY JACK CONNELLY

Cavendish
Square

New York

Published in 2015 by Cavendish Square Publishing, LLC
243 5th Avenue, Suite 136, New York, NY 10016

Copyright © 2015 by Cavendish Square Publishing, LLC

First Edition

No part of this publication may be reproduced, stored in a retrieval system, or transmitted in any form or by any means—electronic, mechanical, photocopying, recording, or otherwise—without the prior permission of the copyright owner. Request for permission should be addressed to Permissions, Cavendish Square Publishing, 243 5th Avenue, Suite 136, New York, NY 10016. Tel (877) 980-4450; fax (877) 980-4454.

Website: cavendishsq.com

This publication represents the opinions and views of the author based on his or her personal experience, knowledge, and research. The information in this book serves as a general guide only. The author and publisher have used their best efforts in preparing this book and disclaim liability rising directly or indirectly from the use and application of this book.

CPSIA Compliance Information: Batch #WS14CSQ

All websites were available and accurate when this book was sent to press.

Library of Congress Cataloging-in-Publication Data

Connelly, Jack.
Discovering Mission San Rafael Arcángel / Jack Connelly.
pages cm. — (California missions)
Includes index.
ISBN 978-1-62713-058-5 (hardcover) ISBN 978-1-62713-060-8 (ebook)
1. Mission San Rafael Arcangel—History—Juvenile literature. 2. Spanish mission buildings—California—San Rafael—History—Juvenile literature. 3. Franciscans—California—San Rafael—History—Juvenile literature. 4. Ohlone Indians—Missions—California—San Rafael—History—Juvenile literature. 5. Miwok Indians—Missions—California—San Rafael Region—History—Juvenile literature. 6. California—History—To 1846—Juvenile literature. I. Title.
F869.M66665C48 2015
979.4'62—dc23
2014003427

Editorial Director: Dean Miller
Editor: Kristen Susienka
Copy Editor: Cynthia Roby
Art Director: Jeffrey Talbot
Designer: Douglas Brooks
Photo Researcher: J8 Media
Production Manager: Jennifer Ryder-Talbot
Production Editor: David McNamara

The photographs in this book are used by permission and through the courtesy of: Cover photo by Mariusz S. Jurgielewicz/Shutterstock.com; © Dee Jolie/Alamy, 1; Richard Cummins/Lonely Planet Images/Getty Images, 4; Edward S. Curtis/File:Hupa Sweat House.jpg/Wikimedia Commons, 7; Courtesy CMRC, 8; Marilyn Angel Wynn/Nativestock/Getty Images, 10; © 2014 Pentacle Press, 12; Courtesy of UC Berkeley, Bancroft Library, 13; Courtesy of UC Berkeley, Bancroft Library, 15; Courtesy of UC Berkeley, Bancroft Library, 16–17; © Karin Hildebrand Lau/Alamy, 18; Charles Deering McCormick Library of Special Collections, Northwestern University, 20; John Stanton/File:Mission San Rafael - 23.jpg/Wikimedia Commons, 22; Sxmuelfernandez/File:Feria del Atole.JPG/Wikimedia Commons, 24; Library of Congress Prints and Photographs Division, 27; Charles Deering McCormick Library of Special Collections, Northwestern University, 29; © North Wind/North Wind Picture Archives, 30; Courtesy of UC Berkeley, Bancroft Library, 32; Stock Montage/Archive Photos/Getty Images, 34; © Bill Helsel/Alamy, 36; Library of Congress Prints and Photographs Division, 41.

Printed in the United States of America

CALIFORNIA
MISSIONS

Contents

1 A New World 5

2 The Miwok and Ohlone 7

3 The Mission System 11

4 From Hospital to Mission 14

5 The First Years of the Mission 19

6 Daily Life at Mission San Rafael Arcángel 23

7 A Mission in Peril 27

8 Secularization 31

9 The Mission Today 35

10 Make Your Own Mission Model 37

Key Dates in Mission History 42

Glossary 44

Pronunciation Guide 45

Find Out More 46

Index 48

Mission San Rafael is one of the youngest missions of California, built in 1821. It stands today as a reminder to all of a transformative time in California's history.

1
A New World

In 1949, architects in San Rafael, California, began to build a **replica** of Mission San Rafael Arcángel, the twentieth mission to be built in a twenty-one-mission chain set up along the coast of California between 1769 and 1823. Mission San Rafael Arcángel stands as an impressive church today, but at one point it was so small it was not even considered a mission. This is the story of Mission San Rafael Arcángel—an important chapter in the story of the missions of California.

EXPLORING OVERSEAS

The story of the California missions began in Spain. In the late 1400s, Spanish explorers began crossing the wide Atlantic Ocean. The Spaniards were quickly joined in their explorations by other newcomers from Britain, France, and the Netherlands. It was a long and dangerous voyage, but they discovered a new continent. Some voyagers came in search of gold, some came to spread their religion, and some came to escape the hardships or persecution they had faced in their homelands. However, the Spanish were responsible for settling the largest area of land in what became known as the **New World**. The Spanish called their land New

Spain, which encompassed what we know today as Mexico and the southwest United States.

It was a long time before Spain decided to explore California. Juan Rodríguez Cabrillo first discovered the area now known as California in 1542. However, the Spanish were not very interested in settling the land. The first explorers did not find any gold or rivers and did not think California would help with their expansion goals. Another problem was misinformation. Many Spanish explorers, including Sebastián Vizcaíno, only knew about the southern tip of California, and believed that it was an island. It was a while before explorers discovered that the island was actually the *Baja*, or "lower," California peninsula.

PRESSURE TO EXPAND

Eventually, King Carlos III of Spain heard that Russian explorers and fur traders were coming from the north to settle the land. The king realized that California was too important for Spain to lose. He wanted to keep the land because it was **fertile** and near the sea. It was a perfect place to build towns and harbors for ships.

Spain was also motivated to expand into California by the Catholic Church. When European explorers first discovered California, many people were already living there. People of the Ohlone, Miwok, and other Native American tribes had established societies and lived throughout California. However, many Spanish believed that the **indigenous people** who lived in California needed to become Christian. **Missionaries** set out from Spain to change the beliefs of the Native Americans in California.

2
The Miwok and Ohlone

THE REAL FIRST SETTLERS

As the Spanish explored what is now California, they found a land populated with more than 100 different tribes of indigenous people. These groups each had their own customs and languages, and were spread throughout the land. Finding many of them near the coastal waters, the Spanish named them *Costeños*, which means the People of the Coast. The primary tribe in the area of Mission San Rafael Arcángel was the Coast Miwok, but there were also Ohlone in the area as well.

A ritual both the Miwok and the Ohlone shared was to cleanse their bodies in sweathouses, similar to this one, called *temescals*.

THE HUNTER-GATHERER LIFESTYLE

The Coast Miwok and Ohlone were hunter-gatherers, which means they lived by hunting, fishing, and gathering food. They hunted game, such as rabbit, deer, and bear. They built traps and decoys to catch birds and other animals to eat. Fish was also an important food for these coastal tribes. They gathered oysters, crabs, and clams. They also ate wild plants and seeds, especially acorns.

Before a hunt, Coast Miwok and Ohlone hunters would cleanse their bodies of odors that might frighten their prey. They did this in a *temescal*, or sweathouse, that produced heat instead of steam. Temescals were considered places of cleansing and healing. After sweating, hunters would jump into an icy stream. This

The Miwok hunted for and gathered their food. Women usually did the cooking, but preparing food was also a social event involving many people from the village.

process also helped to loosen up a hunter's muscles for the chase. Finally, hunters rubbed their bodies and their clothes with mugwort, a plant that smells like mint.

The Ohlone used a technique called slash-and-burn to increase the fertility of the land. Once a year, the Ohlone would start a fire and burn wide-open spaces. Burning the land put many nutrients in the soil, and made it easier for plants that the Ohlone used for food to grow. These controlled fires also helped prevent dangerous wildfires by getting rid of brush.

Gathering and preparing food was a social and fun part of everyday life. The acorn harvest was so important to the Ohlone that it marked the beginning of the year for them. They measured time in terms of how many moons had passed since the last harvest, or how many led up to the next harvest. The acorn harvest was also a main social event for the Ohlone. Several villages would meet to take part in dancing, trading, and feasting.

BUILDINGS

The Coast Miwok and the Ohlone built their villages along bays or rivers that led to the sea. The smallest villages had about twenty people, while the largest had up to 500 inhabitants. Miwoks and Ohlones built their houses from reeds, willow branches, grass, and brush. Their houses were circular, with a hole at the top to let in light and let out smoke from a central fire. Outside their villages, they left mounds of shells as high as 30 feet (9.1 meters) from what they had gathered and eaten. These mounds can still be seen today.

TRADING

The Ohlone and Coast Miwok often traded with each other, and with other tribes throughout California. When the Spaniards first came, they also wanted to trade with the Californians to obtain their handcrafted goods. For example, the Ohlone and Miwok were particularly skilled at basket weaving, and the Spaniards would trade food and other goods for their baskets. These baskets were woven in all shapes and sizes, and some of them were woven so tightly they could even hold water. The baskets were decorated with beads made from abalone shells. These shells were also used as money all over California.

Abalone shells acted as decoration and valuable trading items to the Ohlone.

3
The
Mission System

EXPANDING SPAIN'S REACH INTO CALIFORNIA

The Spaniards built missions throughout the Americas as a way to take control of an area and make the local people into Spanish citizens and Christians. It was decided that a chain of missions and *presidios*, or forts, would be set up along the coast of California. To found each mission, the Spanish government sent two religious leaders called **friars**, or *frays* in Spanish, and several soldiers and military leaders. Fray Junípero Serra founded the first California mission in San Diego on July 16, 1769.

Fray Serra and other missionaries believed it was their Christian duty to bring their religion to the Native Californians. However, the Spanish government had another reason for the mission system. The people who **converted** to Christianity were called **neophytes**, and they could be taxed as citizens of Spain, which helped Spain keep its hold on the land. To ensure this, the California missions were built on the best farming land available. The Spanish missionaries thought that once the indigenous people learned the European way of life, the land could be returned to the neophytes as Spanish citizens. Many people converted. Nevertheless, later events prevented the lands from being returned.

From 1769 to 1823, the Spaniards built twenty-one missions along the coast of California. Small towns developed near or around the missions. More and more settlers came to California. The struggle for control of the **territory** would last for many years and involve Spain, Russia, Mexico, and the United States. For many years, the mission chain gave Spain the strongest foothold in California.

The area where San Rafael is located, between Sonoma and San Francisco, was the focus of much of this international power

The twenty-one missions of California were built along the coast, all connected by a road called *El Camino Real.*

After the Spanish arrived, many parts of Native culture, like the Miwok's acorn granaries, became forgotten over time.

struggle. It would also be the area where the Americans would later stake their claim on California during the Bear Flag Revolt.

For the Coast Miwok and Ohlone, these power struggles meant their old way of life was gone. Their culture was forever changed with the introduction of the mission system. These changes and consequences would continue long after the last mission was abandoned.

The mission system had both strengths and weaknesses. Many Native Californians suffered cruel treatment, especially at the hands of the Spanish soldiers who came with the missionaries to build and protect mission **settlements**. However, many Spanish friars and indigenous people found ways to live and work together in mission communities that were successful both socially and economically, even though they came from very different cultures. For a time, Mission San Rafael Arcángel was one such **community**.

4
From Hospital to Mission

HOSPITAL BEGINNINGS

The original purpose of Mission San Rafael Arcángel was to serve as a hospital. The Europeans brought with them a number of diseases, including measles, smallpox, and flu, that the Native Americans had never been exposed to. This lack of contact meant that the Natives had no immunity to these diseases, so they hit the Natives harder than they did the Europeans, and were often deadly. The cold, damp, and humid climate in the area also slowed the recovery of the sick. Mission San Rafael Arcángel was first a hospital, and then an *asistencia*, or sub-mission of Mission San Francisco de Asís. Located near San Francisco, Mission San Francisco de Asís was also known as Mission Dolores. The Natives did not want to become sick, so many deserted Mission Dolores.

A HEALTHY ENVIRONMENT

President Fray Vicente Francisco Sarría wanted to establish a hospital asistencía to help the sick from Mission Dolores. The friars needed a dry place away from the cold so that people could rest and get better. Lieutenant Gabriel Moraga from the San Francisco presidio chose an area that the Native Californians called Nanaguanui, located north of San Francisco Bay. This was a warm spot, with plenty of sunshine and hills that gave protection from wind and fog.

Although an ideal location had been found, Sarría was worried that he did not have enough priests to work at a new asistencía, so another missionary, Fray Luis Gil y Taboada, offered to help. On December 14, 1817, Fray Taboada, Fray Sarría, and two other friars, Fray Narciso Durán and Fray José Ramon Abella, set off with 200

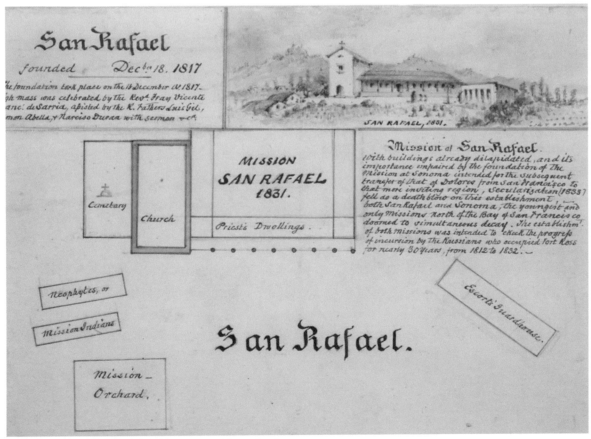

Mission San Rafael began as a sub-mission, or *asistencia*, to Mission San Francisco de Asís.

Miwok and Ohlone to create a place for the sick to be treated.

That afternoon, Fray Sarría baptized twenty-six Miwok and Ohlone children. The friars led the neophytes in song, and **Mass** was held in both the neophytes' native language and in Spanish. They named the asistencía San Rafael Arcángel, after the patron saint of healing. It became the first sanitarium, or a hospital for long-term recovery, in California.

Unlike the cold, foggy environment of Mission Dolores, San Rafael Arcángel had a much healthier climate, with many water sources close by. Fray Taboada had a strong understanding of basic medicine and took good care of his patients. People who came to San Rafael Arcángel soon began to get better. Word of this spread quickly, and soon other missions began sending their sick to the new hospital.

BUILDING THE MISSION

With the growing numbers of newly healthy neophytes, Fray Taboada began expanding the asistencia. He understood much of the Miwok and Ohlone languages, and worked closely with the neophytes on construction of an **adobe** building. Adobe bricks were made from mud and straw and were used because of their ability to keep a house cool in the summer and warm in the winter. Soon, a simple adobe structure 87 feet long (27 m) by 42 feet wide (13 m) housed the hospital, chapel, **granary**, and the living quarters for the friars. Along the side of the building was a corridor covered with **tule**, a reed that is native to California.

Within the first year, the asistencia had grown to a population of more than 300. The hospital was becoming an important part of missionary work in California. Still, San Rafael was not yet an

San Rafael Arcángel asistencia had a better climate than Mission San Francisco de Asís, and many people who were ill were sent there to improve their health.

independent, full-fledged mission—it was still only an asistencía of Mission Dolores. It received food and building supplies from Mission Dolores, and any converts who joined San Rafael as well as the produce grown there technically were a part of Mission Dolores.

RECOGNITION AS A MISSION

People continued to recover from their illnesses at San Rafael Arcángel. After a few years, most of the people at the asistencía were not there for medical help, and very few of the new converts had come originally from Mission Dolores. The purpose of San Rafael Arcángel began to change.

The asistencía started focusing on being self-sufficient so that San Rafael Arcángel would no longer have to depend on Mission Dolores for supplies. The neophytes began farming and taking care of **livestock**. They raised cattle, sheep, and horses, and farmed fields of wheat, barley, corn, and beans. A large vineyard and a pear orchard were created as well.

Mission San Rafael is remembered today by this plaque in the capital of Sacramento.

In 1822, San Rafael Arcángel was officially recognized as an independent mission. It was the smallest mission founded, and one of the last, but it was also one of the most efficient. The farming was very successful and kept people well fed. By the end of the mission, Mission San Rafael Arcángel would convert 1,873 new members, and perform 1,902 marriages.

5
The First Years of the Mission

A NEW LEADER

In 1825, two years after Mission San Rafael Arcángel became independent, Fray Juan Amorós took Fray Taboada's place. He was so successful at running Mission San Rafael Arcángel that within another three years, the mission community grew to more than 1,000 people.

Fray Amorós was a man who took his religious studies seriously. As a missionary, he was very well respected both by other **Franciscan** friars and by the neophytes. One Spanish general in California described Fray Amorós as "a model of virtue, charity, humility, and Christian meekness." It was often said that he carried his lunch in his sleeve—usually an ear of dry corn, roasted over coals. He would eat it slowly as he gave directions to the neophytes at work.

Fray Amorós traveled among the Coast Miwok and Ohlone villages near the mission to encourage the people there to become neophytes. He covered a lot of territory and, in spite of the possible dangers, usually had very little protection with him.

Fray Amorós served Mission San Rafael Arcángel for thirteen of its seventeen years. As well as being remembered for his simple way of living, he will also be remembered for making the most of Mission San Rafael Arcángel.

DIFFERING BELIEFS AND CONVERSION

The missionaries believed that their duty was to spread the Christian religion. However, both the Coast Miwok and Ohlone had their own religious beliefs. The Miwok lived close to nature, so nature played a big part in their religion. They believed in spirits that lived in animals, plants, the earth, the sky, and water. Celebrations and prayers centered on births and marriage, as well as food and other resources.

The Ohlone had a complex belief system as well. They believed that the world was created through

The natural world was very important to the Miwok people. They treated all living things with respect and believed that certain animals should not be harmed.

a battle between good and evil, and that three sacred animals—the hummingbird, the coyote, and the eagle—joined together to create humanity. Many stories and lessons focused around the coyote, which was considered the leader of the animal world.

Although the mission system produced many problems between the Spaniards and the Californians, many positive relationships between the friars and the Coast Miwok and Ohlone were formed at Mission San Rafael Arcángel. Fray Taboada and Fray Amorós taught them Spanish methods of **agriculture**, brickmaking, and other skills, as well as Christian songs for church services. They truly believed that they were helping the local people by teaching them about European culture and converting them to Christianity. They were often kinder and gentler leaders than the soldiers.

BUILDINGS AT THE MISSION

The mission complex was made up of a hospital, a chapel, a storeroom, and a *monjerío* to house unmarried women and girls. Married women lived with their families in the *ranchería*, in homes that were built outside of the mission buildings. Mission San Rafael Arcángel also had a cemetery, a guardhouse, and orchards.

The chapel and other mission buildings at Mission San Rafael Arcángel were very plain. They did not have the beautiful ornaments, designs, or paintings that could be found at the other missions. Unlike other mission buildings, Mission San Rafael Arcángel's church had no tower. Instead, the bells were hung in a group from crossbeams in front of the chapel entrance.

RINGING BELLS

Bells were very important at the missions. They not only made a beautiful sound, but their ringing alerted everyone when it was time to be at work or prayer. Neophyte boys also rang the bells on important occasions, such as when a baby was baptized or when a friar from another mission came to visit. As important as the bells were to mission life, they were also very expensive. The Franciscan friars salvaged one of Mission San Rafael Arcángel's bells from an American whale ship. You can still see the bells at the mission museum today. They have been preserved as a reminder of the way life was at the mission long ago.

Mission San Rafael's original bells are on display at the mission today.

6
Daily Life at Mission San Rafael Arcángel

STARTING THE DAY

The daily routine at the mission began with everyone waking at dawn and then going to Mass. A breakfast, generally hot chocolate and *atole*, or cooked ground corn, followed the service. Atole was a staple of most meals. The rest of the morning was spent doing chores, like caring for the animals or cleaning.

The midday meal was generally eaten in the hour before noon. Prepared by the neophytes, it usually featured atole again, often with either mutton or beans. The old and sick also were served milk with their meal.

A LIFE OF WORK AND PRAYER

The men spent much of the day working in the fields. They herded the cattle, horses, and sheep. When the harvest season was over, they made adobe bricks from soil mixed with water and straw or made tiles from clay.

Atole was a corn-based dish eaten at the mission during mealtimes.

Inside their quarters, the women weaved. They produced all the cloth used at the mission, including blankets, sheets, tablecloths, towels, and napkins.

Work stopped around noon for *siesta,* or a period of rest, and began again around 2:00 p.m. The end of the workday came at 5:00 p.m., and at 6:00 p.m., the evening meal was eaten. At this time, the neophytes would often add nuts, herbs, and wild berries to their atole. They gathered these in large quantities and stored them away. At sundown, everyone marched to the chapel for prayer. There they sang the *Angelus,* a Catholic prayer set to music, and an evening blessing was given. Three times a day, at morning, noon, and night, the bells called everyone to recite the Angelus devotion. At 8:00 p.m., women went to bed. Men went to bed at 9:00 p.m.

LEARNING TO COMMUNICATE

The friars also spent time teaching the neophytes to read and write, not only in Spanish but also in Latin, which allowed them to better understand the Bible. The neophytes also taught the friars to speak the languages of their tribes. The friars heard **confession**, a Catholic ritual in which a person confesses his or her sins to a priest, in the neophytes' own languages.

The government of New Spain wanted all missionaries to learn the different local languages, but not everyone was able to follow this rule. Often it was difficult for the friars to learn the many different languages they heard.

Saturdays were sometimes workdays, but on Sundays and holidays, everyone was allowed to rest and play after a few hours of prayer. Sunday was also a day for trading. Tribes from the surrounding area would come to Mission San Rafael Arcángel to trade goods. In time, some of them also converted and came to live at the mission.

GAMES AND CHILDHOOD

In their free time, the Ohlone played different games, using their hands, sticks, or hoops and poles. In one game, a player would throw a few sticks up in the air. Players would guess whether the number of sticks was odd or even. Another person would count to see who had guessed right. The loser would pay white shells to the winner. Beads were also sometimes given as prizes.

The lives of neophyte boys and girls at the mission were very different. At around age eleven, the girls had to leave their mothers and live and work at the *monjerío*, or nunnery. Once they finished their work, they were allowed to visit their families. At night they were locked inside. Girls had to live at the monjerío under strict supervision until they were married.

Neophyte boys were not locked in at night, nor were they forced to stay in during the day. The friars trained the boys to become bell ringers, to sing in the choir, to play the violin, or to be workers.

LEAVING A CULTURE BEHIND

The Coast Miwok and Ohlone lived an orderly life at the mission, but it was very different from the life they had once known. When the first missionaries came, the Miwok and the Ohlone could not foresee that they would lose their freedom, be forced to give up their way of life, and be kept inside the missions. Many neophytes tried to run away from the missions, but the soldiers went after them and brought them back. The soldiers often treated runaway neophytes with cruelty and punished them with whippings or beatings. While such punishments were not uncommon Spanish practice at the time, many friars did not approve of the soldiers using these methods.

Both the neophytes and the Spanish missionaries faced a number of challenges at Mission San Rafael Arcángel. Even though the friars believed they were helping the Miwok and Ohlone, the Natives did not like adapting to the Spanish way of living. These new customs and beliefs often caused the loss of the Native way of life.

7
A Mission in Peril

CULTURES CONFLICT

The conflict between the neophytes and the missionaries at Mission San Rafael Arcángel was happening at other missions as well. The Natives wanted to keep their customs and heritages, but the friars wanted the neophytes to become more like the Spanish, and this led to problems between the two groups.

The Spanish missionaries and soldiers thought they were doing a good thing by imposing their religion and lifestyle on the Native Americans. Today, we understand that **colonization**

Mission life brought about changes for those living there, which led to conflicts between Native people, friars, and soldiers.

is an unfair practice that unjustly takes land and liberty away from people. We realize today that it is unfair to assume that one culture is superior to, or better than, another culture. Looking back on the mission system, we can see that, in spite of the good intentions, it was harmful and hurtful to many indigenous people. It forced them to give up their culture and values, and it was a violation of their civil rights.

While we can look back at historical events today and clearly see the injustice, it was not so easy for the Spaniards to see it when they were settling in early California. Some of the Coastal Miwok and Ohlone **adapted** to the new way of life the Spaniards brought, but many others did not want to accept these changes. Those who did not want to change their beliefs were nonetheless forced to stay at the missions and give up their old way of life. As their imprisonment continued, they began to feel more and more hopeless. Some tried to run away. Others took a different kind of action.

Sometimes indigenous people attacked the missions. Fray Amorós was always very watchful of attacks by the local people. He had guards on the lookout all the time. During one attack, Fray Amorós was saved from harm by the neophytes. They took him to a hiding place and, to protect him, formed a human wall around him.

The Native Americans who wanted to end the mission system fought against the neophytes who liked the friars. When the attack finally ended, the survivors, including Fray Amorós, returned to Mission San Rafael Arcángel. They discovered that the mission had been damaged and robbed. Fray Amorós and the neophytes began the task of cleaning up the debris.

A Coast Miwok named Pomponio, who came from the area of Mission San Rafael Arcángel, raided the countryside as far south as Mission Santa Cruz. He left a trail of robberies, fights, and murders. The violence was usually directed against other Native people. He was finally captured after killing a soldier.

ENDING THE MISSION?

In spite of its successes, Mission San Rafael Arcángel's importance was always questioned by the church leaders. In 1823, a plan to convert more of northern California called for both Missions San Rafael Arcángel and Dolores to be closed. It was thought that a "new San Francisco" should be built to replace them at nearby Sonoma. Fray Amorós worked hard to defend his mission from this threat.

The destruction of Mission San Rafael Arcángel was delayed because of Fray Amorós's protests. To help hold off the mission's destruction, ninety-two neophytes from Mission San Rafael Arcángel had to be transferred to the new

Some Native people who joined the missions accepted the Spanish way of life and religion.

community at Sonoma. As always, the neophytes were treated as commodities, or products, to be traded. This practice was not uncommon at the time. Today this would be considered slavery, a serious and unacceptable violation of people's civil rights.

A CHANGE FOR THE WORSE

When Fray Amorós died in 1832, a new senior friar took over the running of Mission San Rafael Arcángel. The new senior friar, Fray José Maria Mercado, was a Zacatecan from Mexico. Unlike the previous leaders of San Rafael Arcángel, he was an angry,

In 1834, General Mariano Vallejo took over Mission San Rafael and moved resources like animals and plants to his own ranches.

violent man, and treated the Miwok and Ohlone cruelly. At one point, he armed a group of neophytes and ordered them to kill a group of local people. Twenty-one people were killed and several more were injured. The Church was horrified. This only turned more people against the missions. However, even though what Mercado did was brash and wrong, he was only suspended from mission work for six months as punishment for it.

8
Secularization

VALLEJO TAKES CONTROL

The Mexican people became independent from Spain in 1821. The new nation also gained control of California, including the twenty-one missions. The Mexican government took the missions away from the Franciscans and the Catholic Church, starting with Mission San Rafael Arcángel in 1834. With San Rafael Arcángel only achieving official mission status in 1822, it had one of the shortest lifespans in the California mission system.

In 1834, the Mexican government took control of the mission land from the priests in a process called **secularization**. A Mexican general named Mariano Vallejo was sent to take control of the mission. General Vallejo wanted to own Mission San Rafael Arcángel completely, but Fray Mercado strongly resisted General Vallejo's attempts to control it. Vallejo had his chance, however, when Fray Mercado was suspended from his mission work. The Mexican government gave Vallejo control over all of the mission's resources. Immediately, he moved all the mission's cattle, as well as equipment, supplies, and even vines and fruit trees, to his own ranches. With Mission San Rafael Arcángel now abandoned, he gave the neophytes no other choice but to work for him. As at the

Many neophytes previously living and working at Mission San Rafael were forced to work for General Vallejo as slaves—some of them at his flour mills.

missions, the neophytes were not paid, and they received nothing for their work but room and board.

In 1834, Mission San Rafael Arcángel was grouped with the Sonoma and San Francisco missions and turned into a **parish**, an area with its own church led by a pastor. The land, which the Catholic Church had promised to the neophytes, was instead given or sold to Mexican ranchers. Most of the neophytes went to work on the ranches, where they were treated as slaves. Other neophytes, however, left the area to make it on their own and fared well in their newfound freedom. Some even became businessmen and landowners.

A NEOPHYTE'S SUCCESS

The most successful Coast Miwok in the San Francisco Bay area was Camilo Ynitia, a former neophyte. When the Mexican government took control of the California missions, he was given a land grant of 8,877 acres (3,592.4 hectares). He was the only full indigenous person in Marin County to receive a land grant. He gave the land its name, *Olompali*, making it one of the few places in Marin County to keep its Native name.

When Americans started migrating west to California, Ynitia decided to sell his land to them. At a time when other indigenous families were being robbed of their lands, Ynitia walked away with his money.

CONFLICT WITH CALIFORNIOS: THE BEAR FLAG REVOLT

Until 1840, there were only a small number of Americans in California. Most of them were sailors, traders, or adventurers. After 1840, however, large numbers of Americans headed west in wagon trains. For several years, these Americans made Mexican leaders in California angry. There were fights between the Americans and the *Californios*, or California settlers of Mexican descent. Then for twenty-five days in 1846, Sonoma, just north of San Rafael, became the capital of the independent Republic of California.

A rumor had been spreading that Mexico was planning to throw the *Americanos* out of California. Americanos were non-Mexican settlers from the East Coast of America. At dawn on June 14, 1846, thirty-three heavily armed Americans gathered at the fortress home of General Vallejo. They pounded on the door and demanded that General Vallejo surrender the fortress to them. He welcomed three of them in and, after a meal, they arrested him. Then they raised a new flag, which had a bear, a star, and the words "California Republic" on it. Today the Bear Flag still flies over the state capital of California in Sacramento. This flag also gave the conflict its name. It would go down in history as the Bear Flag Revolt.

Captain John C. Fremont led the American forces that captured San Rafael. The United States were soon handed the rest of the San Francisco Bay area as well. The U.S. Navy sailed to California and raised the flag over Monterey. California was part of the United States in 1848.

John C. Fremont raises the flag of the California Republic as California settlers declare their independence from Mexico.

9
The Mission Today

A PLACE TO LEARN HISTORY

In 1861, the buildings of Mission San Rafael Arcángel were abandoned, and they were eventually torn down. A San Francisco artist, Felix Adrian Raynaud, created a postcard depicting what he thought the historical Mission San Rafael Arcángel looked like, and when the mission was rebuilt in 1949, it seems that Raynaud's postcard was used as the basis for the reconstructed mission.

Today two star-shaped windows grace the front of the church, inspired by the Carmel Mission. Although the new building is made of stone, we know that the original church was made of adobe, thanks to the records kept by the friars.

Many of the things that made the location so good for Mission San Rafael Arcángel are gone today. There were two small streams that brought freshwater from nearby springs to the mission. Ducks, which once lived in nearby mudflats, were an important source of food. Today, their home has become downtown San Rafael.

Today, people can visit Mission San Rafael Arcángel to learn about the site's rich history. The church next door is also an active parish where anyone can worship. While Mission San Rafael Arcángel was the smallest of the missions and its history was filled with challenges, it still played an important role in the development of California.

Today Mission San Rafael has been restored and exists as an active church and tourist destination.

10
Make Your Own Mission Model

To make your own model of Mission San Rafael Arcángel, you will need:

- thin cardboard
- ruler
- scissors
- X-ACTO® knife (ask for an adult's help)
- red, brown, white, and black poster paint
- glue
- tape
- dry lasagna noodles
- green Styrofoam
- Popsicle sticks
- toothpicks
- miniature bell
- string

DIRECTIONS

Adult supervision is suggested.

Step 1. Use a large piece of cardboard as your base. For the front and back of the church, draw the shape shown here on a piece of cardboard. Cut out your outline. Repeat this step.

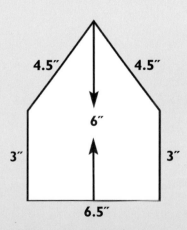

4.5″   4.5″

6″

3″   3″

6.5″

Step 2. Cut two pieces of cardboard to measure 13" × 3" (33 cm × 7.6 cm). These will be the sides of the church.

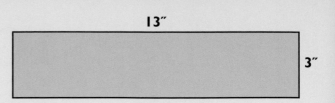

Step 3. Paint all the church walls with white paint. Let dry.

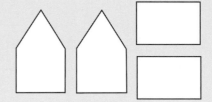

Step 4. To build the friars' quarters, cut two pieces of cardboard to measure 12" × 3" (30.5 cm × 7.6 cm). These pieces are the front and back.

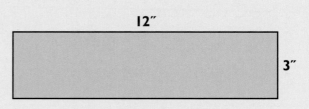

Step 5. Cut two pieces of cardboard to measure 6.5" × 3" (16.5 cm × 7.6 cm). These are the sides of the friars' quarters.

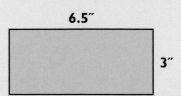

Step 6. Paint the walls of the friars' quarters white. Let dry. Using a pencil, draw where you want doors and windows to be. Do this for the church walls also.

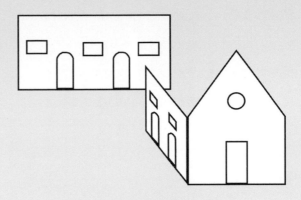

Step 7. Fill in the windows and doors with black paint.

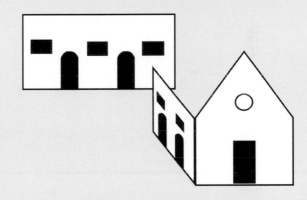

Step 8. Tape the four sides of the church walls together to form a box. Put the tape on the inside, so it doesn't show on the outside of the box.

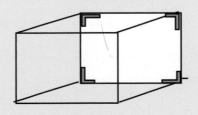

Step 9. Repeat this with the four walls of the friars' quarters to form a box shape.

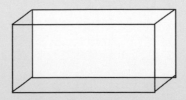

Step 10. Tape both the church and the friars' quarters to your base. Tape the insides only, so the tape doesn't show on the outside.

Step 11. To make the roof of the church, cut a piece of cardboard to measure 13.5" × 9.5" (34.3 cm × 24.1 cm). Bend in half and glue to the top of the church walls.

Step 12. For the friars' quarters roof, cut a piece of cardboard 13" × 8" (33 cm × 20.3 cm). Bend this in half and glue to top of the friars' quarters walls.

Step 13. Paint lasagna noodles with reddish-brown paint. Let dry. Glue to the roofs.

Step 14. Glue two toothpicks together to form a cross. Glue to the roof. Decorate the base with green Styrofoam or other greenery. Add crosses to make a cemetery.

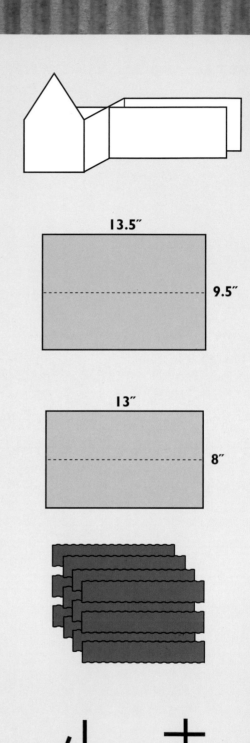

Step 15. Paint Popsicle sticks white. Glue them together as shown below. Tie a string through your miniature bell and hang from Popsicle stick structure. Tape in front of the church.

The completed model of Mission San Rafael Arcángel.

Key Dates in Mission History

1492	Christopher Columbus reaches the West Indies
1542	Cabrillo's expedition to California
1602	Sebastián Vizcaíno sails to California
1713	Fray Junípero Serra is born
1769	Founding of San Diego de Alcalá
1770	Founding of San Carlos Borroméo del Río Carmelo
1771	Founding of San Antonio de Padua and San Gabriel Arcángel
1772	Founding of San Luis Obispo de Tolosa
1775–76	Founding of San Juan Capistrano
1776	Founding of San Francisco de Asís
1776	Declaration of Independence is signed

1777	Founding of Santa Clara de Asís
1782	Founding of San Buenaventura
1784	Fray Serra dies
1786	Founding of Santa Bárbara
1787	Founding of La Purísima Concepción
1791	Founding of Santa Cruz and Nuestra Señora de la Soledad
1797	Founding of San José, San Juan Bautista, San Miguel Arcángel, and San Fernando Rey de España
1798	Founding of San Luis Rey de Francia
1804	Founding of Santa Inés
1817	Founding of San Rafael Arcángel
1823	Founding of San Francisco Solano
1849	Gold found in northern California
1850	California becomes the thirty-first state

Glossary

adapt (uh-DAPT) To change to fit new conditions.

adobe (uh-DOH-bee) Sun-dried bricks made of straw, mud, and sometimes manure.

agriculture (A-grih-kul-cher) Farming.

colonization (kah-luh-nih-ZAY-shun) Claiming land already occupied by other people and bringing new settlers to live there.

community (kuh-MYOO-nih-tee) A group of people who live together in the same place.

confession (kon-FEH-shun) A Catholic ritual in which a person tells his or her sins.

convert (kun-VIRT) To change religious beliefs.

fertile (FUR-til) Being able to produce plants or crops easily.

Franciscan (fran-SIS-kinz) A member of the Franciscan order, a part of the Catholic Church dedicated to preaching, missionaries, and charities.

friars (FRY-urs) Brothers in a communal religious order. Friars also can be priests.

granary (GRAY-nuh-ree) A building where grain is stored.

indigenous people (in-DIJ-en-us PEA-pel) People native to a particular region or environment.

livestock (LYV-stahk) Animals raised on a farm or ranch.

Mass (MAS) A Christian religious ceremony.

missionary (MIH-shun-ayr-ee) Someone who is sent to spread his or her religion in another country.

neophyte (NEE-oh-fyt) The name for a Native American once he or she was baptized into the Christian faith.

New World (NOO WURLD)
What the Europeans once called the combined areas of North, South, and Central America.

parish (PAR-ish) An area with its own church and minister or priest.

replica (REH-plih-kah) A copy of something that looks just like the original.

secularization (seh-kyuh-luh-rih-ZAY-shun) A process by which the mission lands were made to be nonreligious.

settlements (SEH-tuhl-ments) Small villages or groups of houses.

territory (TEHR-ih-tor-ee) A big area of land.

tule (TOO-lee) A reed used by the Californians to make houses and boats.

Pronunciation Guide

asistencias (ah-sis-TEN-see-uhs)

atole (ah-TOH-lay)

fray (FRAY)

monjerío (mohn-hay-REE-oh)

Ohlone (oh-LOH-nee)

ranchería (rahn-cheh-REE-ah)

siesta (see-EHS-tah)

temescal (TEH-mes-kal)

Find Out More

To learn more about the California missions, check out these books, websites, and videos:

BOOKS

Bibby, Brian. *The Fine Art of California Indian Basketry*. Berkeley, CA: Heydey, 2013.

Gibson, Karen Bush. *Native American History for Kids*. Chicago, IL: Chicago Review Press, 2010.

Padelsky, Londie. *California Missions*. Ketchum, ID: Stoecklein Publishing, 2006.

Weber, Francis J. *Blessed Fray Junípero Serra: An Outstanding California Hero*. Bowling Green, MO: Editions Du Signe, 2008.

Williams, Jack S. *The Miwok of California*. New York, NY: PowerKids Press, 2004.

———. *The Ohlone of California*. New York, NY: PowerKids Press, 2003.

Young, Stanley. *The Missions of California*. San Francisco, CA: Chronicle Books, 2004.

WEBSITES

California Missions Resource Center

www.missionscalifornia.com

This website gives essential facts about each mission. It also provides a timeline and a photo gallery.

Mission San Rafael

www.saintraphael.com

This website is the official webpage for Mission San Rafael and its church. It gives information about the mission's history and what it's like today.

San Diego History Center

www.sandiegohistory.org

This website is part of the San Diego history center. It provides articles from its magazine, *The Journal of San Diego History*, including articles about the missions.

VIDEO

Adams, R. J. *The Missions of California*. Laguna Hills, CA: Shannon & Company, 2007. DVD, 60 min.

Index

Page numbers in **boldface** are illustrations.

adapt, 26, 28
adobe, 17, 23, 35
agriculture, 21

colonization, 27
confession, 25
convert, 11–12, 14, 18, 21, 25, 29

disease, 14

explorers
  Cabrillo, Juan Rodríguez, 6
  Vizcaíno, Sebastián, 6

fertile, 6
Franciscan, 19, 22, 31
friars
  Abella, Fray José Ramon, 15
  Amorós, Fray Juan, 19, 21, 28–30
  Durán, Fray Narcisco, 15
  Mercado, Fray José Maria, 30–31

Sarría, Vicente Francisco, 14–16
Taboada, Fray Luis Gil y, 15–16

granary, **13**, 17

indigenous people, 6, 7, 11, 13, 28

livestock, 18, 23

Mass, 16, 23
missionary, 6, 11, 13–15, 17, 19–20, 25–27

neophyte, 11, 16–19, 22–26, 28–30, 32–33, **32**
New World, 5

parish, 32, 36

secularization, 31
settlements, 13

temescal, 7–8
territory, 12, 19
tule, 17